I. Forest fans in Munich, 1979.

II. Celebration time: Tony Woodcock (*left*), with Kenny Burns pictured after the 1979 European Cup final.

Nottingham Forest FC

1. Roy Dwight leads the first assault of the 1959 FA Cup final.

Duncan Hamilton

First published 1988 by

Archive Publications Ltd
Carrington Business Park
Urmston
Manchester
M31 4DD

in association with the

Nottingham Evening Post
Foreman Street
Nottingham
NG1 4AB

Production by Richardson Press

ISBN 0-948946-36-9

2. Wally Ardon cost Billy Walker £12,000 from Rotherham in 1949. By then, the centre forward was approaching his 32nd birthday. He scored 25 goals in his first season and a magnificent 36 (a club record) in the following season to push Forest back into the Second Division. In all, he scored 126 times in 181 appearances.

CONTENTS

Foreword by Maurice Roworth

I wasn't fortunate enough to fulfil my schoolboy ambition and play for Nottingham Forest.
But I'm certainly enjoying the next best thing.
I feel privileged to be chairman of the club that has been at the centre of my life ever since I filed through the City Ground turnstiles for the first in the early 1940s to stand on the terraces.
I like to think that the fact I sit in the directors box hasn't changed me.
I am today what I've always been - a supporter. If it didn't break etiquette, I'd still be wearing a red and white scarf and spending three quarters of every match on my feet.
So the only difference nowadays is that I get to see life behind the scenes.
I'm not simply being biased when I say we have one of the best run clubs in the Football League, as well as employing undoubtably the most able manager that the game has ever produced.
In the 1950s, I was an avid admirer of Wally Ardron and Tommy Capel and I'll never forget the May afternoon in 1959 when Billy Walker's side won the FA Cup (I've kept my ticket stub).
But what Brian Clough has achieved at home and abroad - the way he so emphatically put us on the map - is nothing short of incredible.
I'm pleased that a book like this one has been produced as a record of the success he's brought to us.
It's also a testimony to the other great managers and players in our history during the last thirty years or so.
I just think I'd better warn the publishers that we'll be winning a bit more silverware over the next few years.
So be prepared to add a few more chapters to the book when it's re-issued.

Maurice Roworth,
Chairman,
Nottingham Forest

3. Maurice Roworth and Brian Clough.

Foreword by Brian Clough

I can't remember the last time I actually took a photograph.
But I've always preached the importance of collecting them, keeping them and, above all, cherishing them. A photograph is there for evermore. A picture doesn't simply say a thousand words. The image stays in your memory. That's why I've made sure over the years that I've kept whatever photographs I could.
Among the hundreds in my house, there's yours truly on a vaulting horse with two of my mates during national service; there are pictures of my children walking along the front at Blackpool; others of a few goals I happened to score now and again and a few more with the silverware that I've been proud to win for Nottingham Forest.
When I finally retire to do the garden and sit in a deck chair to soak up the sun, I'll be even more pleased that I saved them. The memories will stay intact.
Which is one reason why I'm glad those people who support Nottingham Forest now have a permanent record of our most memorable moments over the last thirty years or so. It's our history and we're rightly proud of it.

Be good,

Brian Clough

4. Sign here: Chairman Maurice Roworth pulls off a family double at the City Ground. He signs Brian Clough and his goal scoring son, Nigel, on new contracts. Also pictured is assistant manager Ron Fenton.

A Man For All Seasons

How many Football League managers can deliver a one-liner as pithily as Groucho Marx? How many have bought their own advertising space around the ground and ordered another board, placed strategically alongside one of the goals, politely requesting: "Gentleman - no swearing please" to push a message across to the terraces? How many are doggedly pursued by television and newspapers to parley on the Government, the National Health Service or whatever issues dominate the day? And who could command such loyalty that even an invitation from the Football Association, short-listing him as a candidate to take charge of England, could provoke a shrewdly worded response from the supporters. This time the sign, placed directly in front of his dug out read: "Brian - No leaving please, The Gentleman."

The man himself has talked people out of suicide. He has talked to raise money to buy wheelchairs; and since he has never been reluctant to say exactly what he thinks, about whatever stirs him, he attracts more column inches and black banner headlines than the Royal Family.

But then no manager is as essentially unconventional as Brian Clough.

The extraordinary, iconoclastic Clough has been everywhere, done virtually everything, and nearly won the lot. He is a distinct one-off.

He happens to listen to Frank Sinatra records while writing out his team sheet (sometimes even singing along); he brings his dog to work; he acts as drinks waiter to the laundry ladies; he is almost permanently dressed in track suit bottoms (which occasionally he rolls up to his knees) and a loose-fitting green sweat shirt. He is splendidly unpretentious and refers to himself uncharitably as 'Big Head".

Most importantly of all, he has proved himself the best manager in the business time and again. The fact that England did not have the sense to appoint

5. The day it all started; January 5th, 1975. Clough arrives at the City Ground to be met by chairman Jim Willmer.

6. Worried by the use of foul and abusive language on the terraces, Brian Clough ordered this sign to be carried around the ground.

him to the post for which he has always been the people's choice is something for which Nottingham Forest ought to be eternally grateful.

He wrote the original book on the art of football management and the notches on the trophy cabinet explain why his arrival, in January 1975, was the turning point so far as the City Ground was concerned. Two League Championships (one of which was with Derby County), two European Cups (he interrupted a family holiday in Crete to win the first) two League Cups, an FA Cup semi final and a reputation for being able to defy even the longest, most daunting odds bear testimony to what the charismatic Clough has achieved as one of the central figures in the domestic game over the last twenty years, more than three quarters of them spent at Forest.

The avuncular Billy Walker was responsible for the only other milestone capable of matching those created by Clough. In 21 years as manager, Walker, at almost 62, crowned what turned out to be his penultimate season before retirement by capturing the FA Cup for the third time in his career. What is more, he did it with ten men for almost an hour of an unforgettably tense final.

The memory of that extraordinary May afternoon at Wembley in 1959 had to sustain Forest for almost two decades until you know who happened along. The breath of fresh air philosophy of Johnny Carey, an urbane, pipe-smoking figure was succinct. "Fizz it about," preached the gentle Carey, and Forest did, through Ian Moore, Joe Baker, Terry Hennessey, the indefatigable Bob McKinlay, et al, and came within four points of winning the Championship and also narrowly lost an FA Cup semi-final in the same season. The promise of the squad adroitly assembled by the softly-spoken manager petered out and Carey was sacked in 1968 when Forest lay joint bottom of the First Division. Carey was non-plussed about the decision - "It doesn't make sense to me." he said, quietly - but typically remained a gentleman to the end. He cleared out his office, promising to improve his golf handicap. "By kind permission of Forest, I now have plenty of time to do it."

Apart from the glittering jewel of Wembley and the so near, yet so far Carey era, Forest had been more familiar with failure than success before Clough. The bare statistics were hardly shattering: formed in 1865; took root at the City Ground (after five different homes) in 1899; and FA Cup winners a year earlier when Derby were skilfully taken apart in front of a 60,000 gate at Crystal Palace. What followed over the next half century was a frustrating string of seasons where relegation followed agonisingly hard on the heels of promotion or when Forest could do no more than consolidate: Second Division Champions 1907; relegated 1911; Second Division winners again 1922; relegated three years later; relegated once more 1949; promotion from Division Three as champions 1951; promotion to Division One (as runners-up) in 1957.

By the time Clough took over - his fourth club in 15 months - Forest were once more in a parlous position; buried in the nether regions of the Second Division and drifting towards the Third. The club had suffered relegation (in 1972, ironically the season in which Clough and assistant manager Peter Taylor were steering Derby County to the Championship)

7. When Clough was being interviewed for the England manager's job, the supporters responded by erecting a placard of their own: Brian - No leaving, please. The Gentlemen.

and had gone through three other managers post-Carey (Matt Gillies, Dave MacKay and Allan Brown, all Scots) before Clough clocked in, courtesy of a lack of patience from Leeds United. Clough's reign at Elland Road had lasted only 44 days, before he was abruptly sacked, scarcely having time to find the gents cloakroom, let alone reshape the then League Champions. Fortunately Clough still lived in Derby and so the move to the City Ground was made-to-measure. It offered him both employment and the chance to prove a few folk spectacularly wrong.

The City Ground was as logical a destination both for Taylor - even though it took until July 1976 to lever him away from Brighton - and for Jimmy Gordon. Taylor, born in the Meadows, came home. Gordon, unfailingly buoyant, was not only automatic choice as coach but he also happened to be Clough's first signing. After reaching a third successive League Cup final, the tribute to Gordon was in unselfishly pushing him down the tunnel to lead Forest out at Wembley, the clearest example of the esteem Clough and Taylor held for him as a coach capable of communicating their ideas with the minimum of fuss. The stock phrase from Clough about how the remarkable, pioneering partnership with Taylor functioned was succinct: "I'm the front window - he's the goods at the back." On that basis, the sign above the store ought to have read: Clough & Taylor, Master Builders Ltd. What the pair achieved at Forest and Derby, with a distinct style and formula others even now vainly strive to copy, was built from nothing. The alliance was unique and not only because of the amount of silver polish Forest unexpectedly had to order between 1978 and 1980. No other management team has been as successful. "There's no secret," said Clough, "Except hard work and talent - and I'm not kidding." Clough and Taylor lent each other moral support, relied on one another's judgment, wheeled and dealed in the transfer market and together had the alchemists touch for 17 seasons, six of them at Forest. Describing his partner, Clough said: "He sees things 24 hours before I do," and he has forever maintained that, apart from Eric Morecambe, only Taylor's sense of humour was capable of making him cry with laughter.

At its peak, the Clough-Taylor-Forest bandwagon was unstoppable. "It got so good that had I told Brian we should sign Arthur Scargill, I honestly think he would have replied that we could do it there and then," said Taylor. There was a discipline and dash about Forest. Starting with the modest, low-profile Anglo-Scottish Cup, then promotion, Wembley, the League Championship and Europe, Forest dominated the landscape both at home and abroad. Along the way, Clough and Taylor sat side-by-side, sharing the credit, through a 42 match unbeaten run in the First Division, a feat never likely to be surpassed; a Charity Shield; two FA Cup quarter-finals; two Super Cups; the buying and selling of £1m players, notably the mould-breaking transfer of Trevor Francis, as well as lightning fast trip to Tokyo (32 hours of flying in four exhausting days) for a World Club Championship final. Champagne became the staple diet for Forest as one success followed another. Sustaining it was more difficult. Those heady days passed by so rapidly that even when the City Ground was attracting gates of substantially more than 30,000, when Wembley was almost automatically written into the fixture list at the beginning of every August and when Europe - stretching from Madrid to Munich and beyond - more or less became a suburb of Nottingham, the real scale of what had happened was, at times, never fully appreciated by a large proportion of the public Clough and Taylor were catering for. Until, of course, the trophies dried up.

For the manager who had reigned supreme, Clough was suddenly caught in the unlikely position of having to prove himself all over again when Taylor decided to retire, prematurely as it turned out, in 1982 because of the "mental and physical strain". The widely-held assumption was that Clough would soon follow him (particularly after a health-scare of his own four months earlier). The theory was wrong. The sequel to Taylor's departure was the sight of Clough, head down, reconstructing his squad on limited resources and digging Forest out of a potentially crippling financial hole. That he managed it and created a new, eloquent team in the process merely adds to the legend. What irks him most these days is frequent specualtion that he is about to quit, a lot of it fuelled for no other reason than his reluctance to commit himself too far into the future. In truth, Clough's motivation is as strong as ever, a point strengthened only last season by his response to being brutally written off before a ball was even kicked and his readiness to become part-time manager of Wales before the World Cup. Using one of his favourite phrases, Clough dismisses the stories about retirement as being "too daft to laugh at" and asks "What would I do?" He even answers the question himself: "I don't know anything apart from my own industry. I like cricket and gardening - but I'm not at the stage of life yet when I want to spend all my time cutting the grass, pottering around the greenhouse or sitting in a deckchair on the boundary. In my case, retirement means not coming back."

When he does eventually go, the game will be a lot duller. Whatever he decides in the coming seasons, expect Brian Clough to do the unexpected.

8. One of the attempts by Derby to lure him back to the Baseball Ground came near the end of the promotion season in 1977. After a day of soul-searching, Clough was driven along the A52 by Jimmy Gordon to tell the then Derby chairman, George Hardy, that he would not be joining them.

9. Brian Clough and Peter Taylor with chairman Stuart Dryden after rejecting the Derby offer.

10-12. *above:* The awards man - with the Championship and League Cups and his reward for winning them in 1978. *above right:* The Manager of the Year Trophy. *right:* Father and son: Nigel Clough ten years before his League debut.

13, 14, 15 & 16. The agony of it all. Four examples of how the dug out can be a lonely place; especially when you're trying to get over a point.

17. Brian Clough picks up his manager of the month award for December 1987. On the same afternoon his goal-scoring son Nigel is given a prize of his own, from a national newspaper for his performances on the field during the same month.

III. The man himself: Brian Clough.

IV. Brian Clough outside a Shinto shrine during Forest's somewhat brief visit to Japan to play the South American side Nacional in the World Cup Championship final.

18. When Clough pledged himself to Forest for another year in January 1987, he insisted that this photograph be taken outside the wire fence surrounding Forest's training ground. "I feel like a prisoner so I may as well look like one," he told *Evening Post* photographer Trevor Bartlett. The inspiration for it arrived the night before when he saw the film *Papillon,* the story of the Frenchman who spent years trying to escape from jail in French Guyana. Sure enough, the *Football Post* ran it across the front page with PRISONER as the headline. After seeing it, Clough added, "I forgot to put my hands on the bars."

19. He didn't need a passport to get into Wales. But the chance of competing in the World Cup vanished when the Forest board refused permission for him to become part time boss of the Welsh after a confusing few days of speculation. This symbolic gesture says it all.

FA Cup Glory: The Path to 59

The FA Cup belonged to Nottingham Forest, along with a piece of history in 1959 - the first team to win it with ten men. Roy Dwight scored the first goal and then had to watch Forest hang on to a 2-1 lead on television while lying in a Wembley hospital, saying later - "I suffered more agony watching the lads fighting it out than I did from my broken leg." A few hours after the final, Dwight had his winners medal delivered to him by a few of his team mates and he absolved Brendan McNally from any blame for the challenge that left him with a cracked shinbone in his right leg: "It was my own fault. I tried to run through and collided with him. It was just one of those things." Dwight added, smiling: "It was such a pity because I scored the goal with my left foot and I was saving my right for the second one."

Forest were two goals in front inside 17 minutes. Forest's first goal came in the eigth minute when Dwight intuitively fastened onto a ball from Stuart Imlach near the fringe of the area. Tommy Wilson stretched the lead, heading in a deadly accurate cross from Billy Gray. Forest dominated the game and threatened to turn the final into a goalkeeper's nightmare; Wilson grazed the post, Dwight went fractionally close and Luton Town were left completely bewildered, groping blindly for an answer. When Dwight was stretchered off shortly after half an hour - "there were tears in my eyes," admitted the manager Billy Walker - it re-opened the argument about substitutes. The only duty the '12th man' Geoff Thomas could perform was to accompany Dwight to hospital (the sixth player to be injured in the previous eight finals). Forest had exerted such an influence over the initial stages that Walker envisaged a performance in the classic mould of the 1928 Wembley Wizards when Scotland overwhelmed England 5-1. Instead, the absence of Dwight almost cost them the Cup. Luton inevitably pulled a goal back in the 62nd minute, and Forest had to sweat it out, survive and finally fulfill the prediction Walker had made before a ball had been kicked in the competition. He sensed it was going to be his year again.

20. The promotion squad of 1956-57: *back row: left to right*: Thomas, McKinlay, Burkitt, Farmer, Barrett, Jones, Watson. *middle row*: Graham, Wilson, Higham, Alexander, Imlach, Lishman, Scott, Walker. *front row*: Small, Whare, Morley. Forest finished second in the table, seven points behind Liverpool.

Walker certainly had the Midas touch in the Cup. He could almost claim part ownership of it winning the trophy three times, once as a player (in his debut season at Aston Villa in 1920) and twice as a manager (the first for Sheffield Wednesday 15 years later). He even took Southern League Chelmsford as far as the fifth round.

Walker began his managerial career at Wednesday (the club were second from bottom of the First Division when he arrived) and promptly won the Cup inside 16 months, walking down the Wembley tunnel afterwards with the lid of the trophy perched on his head. When life at Hillsborough became altogether different four and a half years after his appointment, he resigned and Chelmsford almost instantly offered him the chance to climb back into management. "I felt like an Olympic diving champion," admitted Walker of his drop in status, "who has been condemned to stay at the shallow end."

By the time he became manager of Forest - barely a month after finally deciding that an existence in the Southern League was not for him - it was 1939. A genial man, he suffered relegation to the Third Division exactly ten years later (Leicester City pushed them down) before gaining promotion in 1951 as Third Division Champions (Forest scored a club record of 110 goals, with Wally Ardon getting 35 of them), finally resurfacing in the First Division in 1957. By then Walker had diligently begun assembling his Cup winning side; Imlach was signed from Derby in 1955 followed two years later by Chick Thomson (Chelsea), Billy Gray (Burnley) and Johnny Quigley (from an amateur Scottish side). The summer of 1958 saw Walker move adroitly for Dwight (Fulham), McDonald (Sunderland) and Jeff Whitefoot (Grimsby). The magnificent seven joined Jack Burkitt, Bob McKinlay, Bill Whare and Tommy Wilson, each of them established at the City Ground. Walker was always anxious to dispel what he considered was a dreadful misconception about the squad. After Wembley, he argued: "We've been referred to variously as 'the team of misfits'. The fact is our side was more of a tight fit than a misfit. We make no pretence to be a team of stars. But all of them have got ability - and the same size hats. When I went for them, I did so with a clear picture in my mind of what we needed." The team he steered to the Cup was unchanged throughout the six matches but only managed to finish thirteenth in the table, primarily because of a barren, nervous spell in the build up to the final. They won only three times in thirteen matches, including a 5-1 defeat at Luton when the man who was to become their sixth postwar manager, Allan Brown, got four goals. Hardly an encouraging portent.

Walker was also within a quarter of an hour of being denied his Cup hat-trick in the third round on a frozen, badly rutted surface at Tooting and Mitcham in a tie he insisted ought "never to have been played." (Walker argued afterwards that the ruts in the pitch were responsible for three of the four

21. The path that led to promotion. Sheffield United defenders are scattered and dejected as inside left Doug Lishman completes his hat trick in a 4-0 win at Bramall Lane that returned Forest to the First Division in 1957.

goals). After falling two behind at half-time, an incredulous Forest pulled one back courtesy of an own goal and finally scraped a replay when the phlegmatic Gray rapped in a penalty. Tooting never remotely looked like giant-killers again; Forest crushed them 3-0 in the replay. In the fourth round, Grimsby, beaten 2-1, suffered the same remorseless fate as Tooting. The sweat and toil marathon against Birmingham was completely different. An equaliser by Wilson saved them at St. Andrews with less than a minute to spare; another by Dwight salvaged a second replay as the minutes drained away in extra time at the City Ground. A fatigued and out-classed Birmingham could not contain Dwight a third time. The Midlands rivals were not so much beaten as torn apart in a 5-0 rout, with a hat-trick drilled in by Dwight.

For the quarter-final clash against the Cup holders, Bolton Wanderers, the tactics Walker employed were straightforward and entirely designed to cut out the strength in the air of Nat Lofthouse. The full backs, Whare and McDonald, carried out the Walker plan so effectively that the Lion of Vienna lost his roar. A bemused Lofthouse mustered just one shot and a single header, and Forest won 2-1. The semi-final - against Aston Villa, staged at Hillsborough - can scarcely have been more poignant for Walker. Forest overcame his former club on the ground where he had been manager, through a solitary goal from a neat piece of finishing by Quigley.

Wembley even provided an uncanny coincidence: the referee was called Clough. The final itself merely confirmed Forest as one of the most watchable teams in the country, " There's often a lot of foolish talk about so-called secret plans for defeating this team and that or of winning the Cup," said Walker. " We had a plan to win the Cup. A simple one - to play our normal game." After it was over, Forest went on to a banquet at the Savoy, then spent Sunday in Brighton, where almost the entire team squeezed themselves into a tiny hotel room to see the televised highlights of the final on a 14 inch black and white set. More than 200,000 supporters lined the route for the homecoming to Nottingham. Afterwards, the players arranged their own dance . "I got home around two o'clock in the morning," said Walker. "That wasn't too bad for an old 'un who was proudly showing his Cup medal before most of the team were born." He also reserved a tribute for the Nottingham public. "The return to Nottingham transcended everything I have ever known in the game. The warmth of the welcome was more stirring than anything else I've experienced."

The following season, Forest were knocked out in the fourth round and narrowly escaped relegation, finishing in 20th place only a point ahead of Leeds. Walker retired after 21 years.

22. Tommy Wilson beats Sheffield United's Alan Hodgkinson to claim Forest's second goal.

23. The players celebrate promotion.

24. Forest, incredibly, kept an unchanged team throughout the Cup run. The eleven, relaxing after a training session, are: *back row left to right*: Whitefoot, Wilson, McKinlay, McDonald, Gray, Quigley, Whare. *front row*: Thomson, Dwight, Burkitt, Imlach.

25. How the Cup was almost lost: Forest eke out a 2-2 draw in the third round against Tooting and Mitcham. A shot from Murphy puts Tooting ahead.

26 & 27. *above*: Tommy Wilson sees his header clear the bar on the fro bound pitch. *below*: Wilson scores - this time in the replay at the City Ground.

28 & 29. Bob McKinlay had his testimonial in Forest's Centenary year, 1965. He still holds the record number of League appearances (614, between 1951 and 1970) for the club. For once, he loses out in a duel with Grimsby's Ron Rafferty. Jeff Whitefoot can't bear to look. The fourth round tie was a rout - Forest won 4-1, Wilson grabbing the last goal.

30. Roy Dwight scores the equaliser in the fifth round replay against Birmingham - the second draw in four days - and went on to fire a hat-trick in the second replay.

31. Tommy Wilson puts Forest ahead against Bolton.

32. Thomson knocks a high ball out of Lofthouse's reach.

33. The road to Wembley. Johnny Quigley *(on the floor)* claims the only goal of the semi-final against Aston Villa at Hillsborough. It arrived in the 65th minute.

34. Chick Thomson smothers the ball to deny Sewell.

35. Come on you Reds. Six fans spell out their loyalty.

36. Another quartet smiling down Wembley Way.

37. The goals that won the Cup. Roy Dwight fires home the first.

38. Tommy Wilson heads the second.

39. Forest keeper Chick Thomson watches helplessly as an effort from Don Pacey *(centre)* slips past him. (The Luton player on the left is Allan Brown, who later became Forest manager.)

40. Roy Dwight is stretchered off with a broken leg at Wembley.

41. Jack Burkitt receives the Cup from the Queen.

42. And then turns in traditional fashion to show off the trophy to the Forest supporters.

43. Burkitt being congratulated as he makes his way down those famous 39 steps.

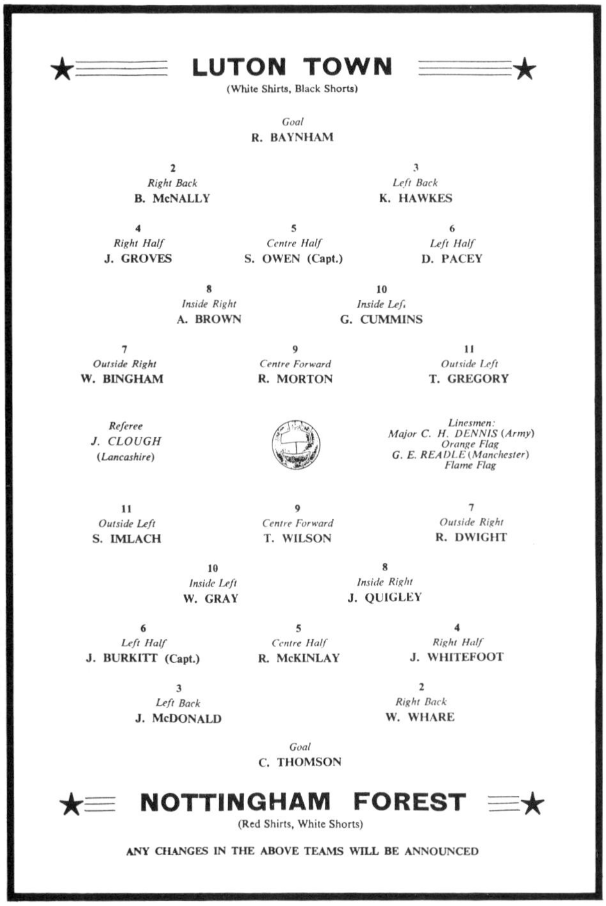
LUTON TOWN
(White Shirts, Black Shorts)

Goal
R. BAYNHAM

2 *Right Back* B. McNALLY — 3 *Left Back* K. HAWKES

4 *Right Half* J. GROVES — 5 *Centre Half* S. OWEN (Capt.) — 6 *Left Half* D. PACEY

8 *Inside Right* A. BROWN — 10 *Inside Left* G. CUMMINS

7 *Outside Right* W. BINGHAM — 9 *Centre Forward* R. MORTON — 11 *Outside Left* T. GREGORY

Referee J. CLOUGH (*Lancashire*)

Linesmen: Major C. H. DENNIS (*Army*) *Orange Flag*; G. E. READLE (*Manchester*) *Flame Flag*

11 *Outside Left* S. IMLACH — 9 *Centre Forward* T. WILSON — 7 *Outside Right* R. DWIGHT

10 *Inside Left* W. GRAY — 8 *Inside Right* J. QUIGLEY

6 *Left Half* J. BURKITT (Capt.) — 5 *Centre Half* R. McKINLAY — 4 *Right Half* J. WHITEFOOT

3 *Left Back* J. McDONALD — 2 *Right Back* W. WHARE

Goal
C. THOMSON

NOTTINGHAM FOREST
(Red Shirts, White Shorts)

ANY CHANGES IN THE ABOVE TEAMS WILL BE ANNOUNCED

PATH TO WEMBLEY

Third round:	Tooting and Mitcham 2, Forest 2 (own goal, Gray penalty)
Replay:	Forest 3 (Dwight, Wilson, Imlach) Tooting and Mitcham 0
Fourth round:	Forest 4 (Gray 2, Whitefoot, Wilson) Grimsby 1
Fifth round:	Birmingham 1 Forest 1 (Wilson)
Replay:	Forest 1 (Dwight), Birmingham 1
Second replay at Leicester:	Forest 5 (Dwight 3, Gray 2) Birmingham 0
Sixth round:	Forest 2 (Wilson 2), Bolton 1
Semi final:	Forest 1 (Quigley), Aston Villa 0
Final:	Forest 2 (Dwight, Wilson) Luton 1 (Pacey)
Forest:	Thomson, Whare, McDonald, Whitefoot, McKinlay, Burkitt, Dwight, Quigley, Wilson, Gray, Imlach
Luton:	Baynham, McNally, Hawkes, Groves, Owen, Pacey, Bingham, Brown, Morton, Cummins, Gregory
Referee:	J Clough

45. Homeward bound. The Nottingham Forest coach inches its way through the crowded streets and then past the central station. The coach had actually arrived less than an hour before the final and was forced to park almost 200 yards from Wembley. "We didn't have time to get nervous - because we had to get changed so quickly" remembered Billy Gray.

46. Even *South Pacific* (a block-buster) takes second billing to Forest at the Odeon.

47. Guard of honour: Jack Burkitt and Billy Walker are given a police escort into the Council House. The policeman looks as though he would have made a useful centre half.

48. Recognise anyone you know? The world and his wife crowd into the Market Square as Forest show off the FA Cup.

49. Roy Dwight is handed the trophy by Jack Burkitt on the Council House balcony.

50. The Cup winners on parade: *back row, left to right*: G Noel Watson, Whare, McDonald, McKinlay, Dwight, Thomson, Whitefoot, Graham. *front row*: Quigley, Gray, Burkitt, Walker, Wilson, Imlach. (Roy Dwight was deliberately placed on the back row and wore track suit bottoms to disguise the fact he was still in plaster when this photograph was taken.)

51. Billy Walker shows off the FA Cup to his 11 year old grand daughter Diane McDevitt. Walker also took the trophy to the Thieves Wood School for Disabled Children. "Seeing them smile made me realise what our win meant," said Walker. "The reaction from the children gave me a better feeling than winning at Wembley."

Forest - The Chase For The League Cup

The headline writers didn't have to put much effort or imagination into their work before Nottingham Forest's first League Cup final. Brian Clough kindly manufactured one for them. His description of Nottingham Forest - "Wembley-wise, most of us are virgins," - did it all. Inside three years, those same Wembley virgins found the place as familiar as their own backyard. The League Cup became such a permanent fixture, that the three-handled trophy almost walked to the City Ground on its own. All this despite the fact Forest won it for the first time with a contentious penalty that Liverpool still argue about even now (with a bit of justification actually) and with a goalkeeper who had not played a solitary League game. Chris Woods was the archetypical Virgin soldier; 18 years and 124 days old when he shut out Liverpool at Wembley and four days older when he did it again in the replay at Old Trafford. But Woods was only half the story of this piece of giant-killing. The bottom line was simply this; the equivalent of Nottingham Forest reserves beat the then First Division and European Champions, as Peter Shilton, Archie Gemmill, and David Needham were all cup tied, and Colin Barrett and John McGovern were both injured. Forest frustrated and finally beat Liverpool, albeit in controversial circumstances. That television proved the foul on John O'Hare was committed a few feet outside the area, detracted not one iota from the achievement. As O'Hare was going clear, anyway, Forest can claim it was morally a penalty irrespective of the protests afterwards of the man who brought him down. Phil Thompson did not attempt to defend the tackle; instead he simply insisted: "It was a professional foul. He was outside the box when I kicked him. I know that sounds bad - but it's the truth". Whatever the arguments, there was no disputing the way John Robertson despatched the penalty with clinical efficiency, striking his effort low and to the right of a vain dive by Ray Clemence. Nor did the furore spoil the fish and chip supper Clough ate at home later that night, with the League Cup perched on top of the television like a matter of fact piece of bric-a-brac. "I'm sure most people don't realise the scope of what we've done," was Clough's succinct appraisal of events. At Wembley, Liverpool created the cleaner cut chances - even putting the ball in the net once, only to be beaten by an off-side flag - and were denied by Woods, revealing no discernible nerves. At Old Trafford, (where Kenny Burns replaced the absent McGovern as captain) Forest were patient and precise, traits that barely a month later would finally secure them the Championship. "All we'd won up until then was the Anglo Scottish Cup," said Clough. "Winning the League Cup gave us the impetus to finish off the job in the Championship." The semi-final was almost as satisfying and certainly a poignant affair for Clough. It provided revenge for him over Leeds. At Elland Road, Forest crushed his former club of 44 days 3-1 and scored another four goals in the second leg.

A year later, the way Forest had become Liverpool's nemesis was emphasised again. Guess who were beaten in the semi-finals to secure another Wembley ticket? Forest had already been back to the twin-towers hotel before the second League Cup final appearance. The season had started there with a goals avalanche against unfortunate Ipswich in the Charity Shield; 5-0 did not flatter Forest and the FA Cup holders were made to look tradesmanlike by comparison. But to retain the League Cup, Clough and Peter Taylor were forced to breathe the sort of half time fire that made the paint peel on the dressing room walls. Forest were trailing to Southampton and, according to Clough, "were treating the final like a practise match". "As the players were ready to go back out of the dressing room, we told them to go down the tunnel running and not to stop until the match was won," explained Taylor. Consequently, the slightly bewildered crowd were treated to the sight of Forest sprinting the thirty or so yards from the mouth of the tunnel on to the pitch. They never stopped for breath until the champagne was opened afterwards; a 3-2 win, two goals to Garry Birtles, thank you very much, and a final to be proud of. A linesman's flag prevented Birtles from scoring four times. "I believe one was offside - but I'll never be convinced about the other. And I've always thought how marvellous it would have been to score a Wembley hat-trick". Forest failed to land a hat trick of their own a year later after yet again removing Liverpool in the semi-finals with two Robertson penalties.

The League Cup treble was there for the taking and Forest did not so much lose the trophy as present it to Wolves, tied in a ribbon. The winner was a slapstick affair; Shilton came for a long, high and thoroughly innocuous through pass and collided agonisingly with Needham near the edge of his area. When the ball struck Needham on the chest, it rolled conveniently to the unmarked Andy Gray, in front of a yawning net. It was a dour, lifeless game, which made surrendering the League Cup all the harder to accept. Shilton took the blame for the goal. "I thought David might struggle to get it away. I yelled that I'd sort it out and he couldn't hear me for the noise of the crowd. It was my fault." Needham was adamant he should share the criticism.

It was the first time under Clough and Taylor that Forest had experienced the acid taste of defeat in the final of major competition and it also ended the sequence of Wembley appearances until 1988. The stadium was a quarter full when Forest won the Mercantile Credit Festival, that much maligned 16 team tournament staged to celebrate the centenary of the Football League.

Just as they had beaten Liverpool ten years earlier, Forest overcame Sheffield Wednesday on penalties.

52. The flooding in the winter of 1946 meant the loss of valuable records, the loan of Meadow Lane and a fixture list that, unbelievably, stretched on into June.

53. In August 1968 Forest were forced to play six matches at Notts County's Meadow Lane ground after a fire engulfed the main stand in a game against Leeds.

54. A face in the crowd; it belongs to John Winfield *(extreme right)* in the thick of the crowd which poured onto the pitch for safety.

55. Johnny Carey examines the wreckage of the Forest fire.

56. An aerial picture taken before the Executive Stand was built.

;7. A century celebrated. To mark the club's :entenary in 1965, Forest staged a City Ground game against Valencia which, ıppropriately enough, ended in a 1-1 draw in ront of an 18,000-plus crowd. Valencia vere hand picked as the opposition after the wo legged affair against them in the Inter Cities Fairs Cup four years earlier (the :ompetition was then only open to cities who staged international fairs; Forest thereby qualified, courtesy of Goose Fair) when the Spaniards beat them 7-1 on aggregate. It vas 1967 before Forest won another European icket, beating Eintract Frankfurt 5-0 before osing to FC Zurich on the away goals rule ıfter drawing 2-2 over the two legs. Bob McKinlay exchanges souvenirs with Valencia :aptain Roberto in 1965. The referee is Bill Clements.

58. Spanish keeper Zamora challenges Frank Wignall, watched by his captain.

59. Chris Crowe pushes his penalty past Zamora to put Forest ahead.

60-61. Forest reached the semi-final of the FA Cup in 1966-67. In the sixth round there was an epic encounter with Everton at the City ground when Ian Moore claimed a memorable hat-trick with a winner in the last minute (*above*). Peter Grummitt cannot prevent a Jimmy Husband goal. In the semi at Hillsborough Forest lost 2-1 to Spurs (who went on to win at Wembley). *below:* Terry Hennessy (out of picture) scores the first goal, squeezing his effort past Pat Jennings.

62-63. *above:* Jimmy Greaves is denied by the fingertips of Peter Grummitt at Hillsborough. *below:* The Carey side which finished runners-up in the Championship (1966-67) and reached the FA Cup semi-final, losing to Spurs. *back row. left to right:* Carey, Hindley, McKinlay, Peter Grummitt, John Winfield, Henry Newton, Tommy Cavanagh. *front row:* Barry Lyons, Joe Baker, John Barnwell, Terry Hennessey, Frank Wignall, Ian Moore.

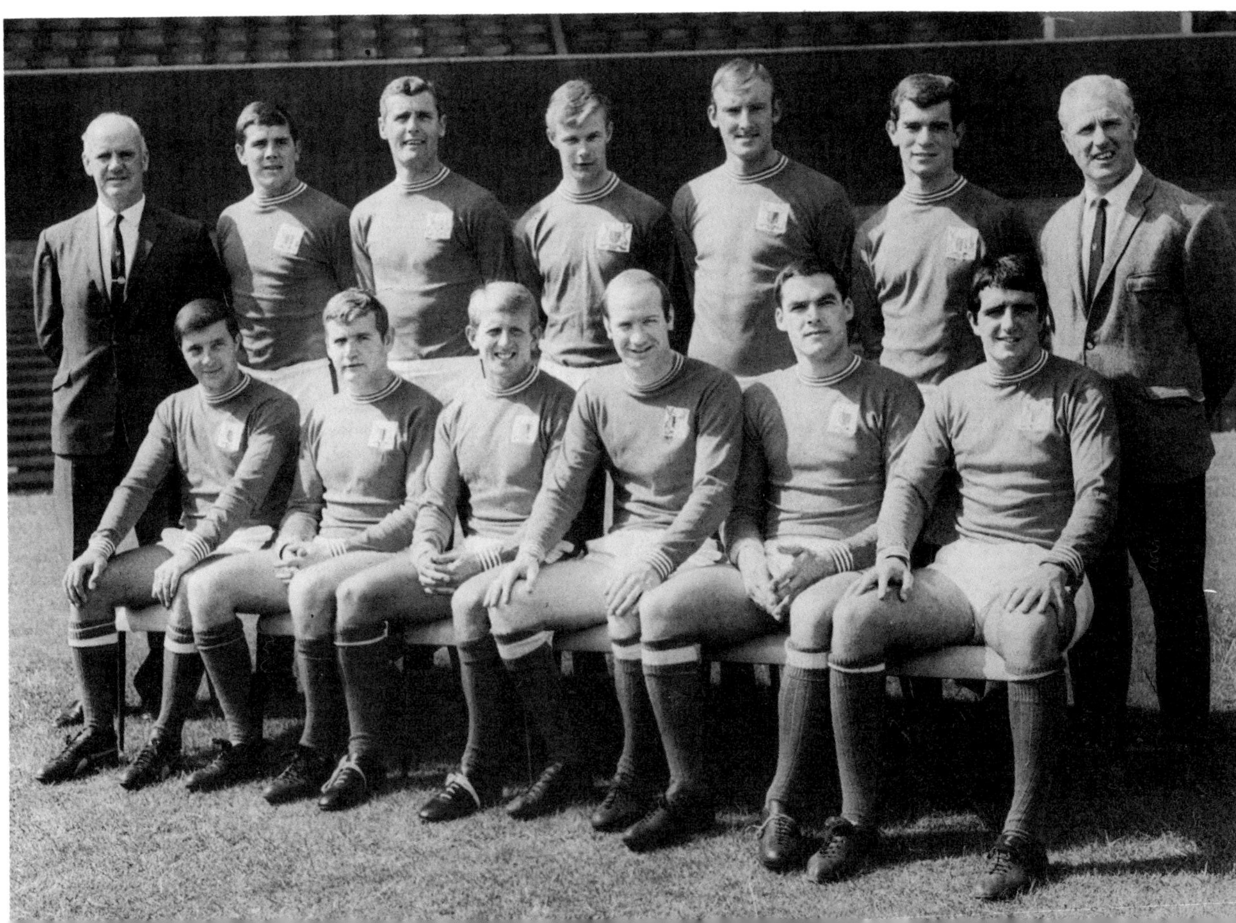

64. Jim Baxter, only three League goals in 48 appearances after being signed for £100,000 exactly twelve months after Baker.

65. Cap this: Terry Hennesey (a £50,000 buy from Birmingham in 1965) and Baker on being awarded international caps. *left to right*: Winfield, Wignall, Hindley, Hennesey, Crowe, Baker, Grummitt, Moore, McKinlay, Barnwell.

66-67. *above left:* In ten years Ian Moore made 236 League appearances (105 goals) before being sold to Manchester United for £200,000-plus. *above right:* The Flying Scotsman - the £60,000 man, zigger zagger Joe Baker - who was bought from Arsenal for a club record fee in 1966 and scored 41 League goals in 116 appearances before being sold to Sunderland.

68. Andy Beattie, a former Scottish international who took Forest to ninth position in the League in his final season at the club.

69. Of the six managers, post Billy Walker and pre Brian Clough, there is no doubt that Johnny Carey was the most successful as well as the longest serving.

70. Carey is interviewed after his sacking.

71. Carey's replacement was Matt Gillies, a former boss at Leicester. He handed a free transfer to Jim Baxter, sold Joe Banker to Sunderland for £50,000, Henry Newton to Everton (£150,000), Terry Hennesey to Derby (£110,000) and was resigned to losing Ian Moore. The transitional period ended in relegation in 1971-72 (the year Derby won the title) and the departure of Gillies.

72. Enter Dave Mackay, albeit for a brief, though productive spell before the acrimonious resignations of Brian Clough and Peter Taylor at Derby propped the door open for him to go to the Baseball Ground.

73. MacKay's successor was Allan Brown, who was unfortunate not to take Forest to an FA Cup semi-final, before you know who was available and promptly recruited.

74. Cup of woe: The FA Cup quarter final against Newcastle at St James Park in March 1974. Forest led 3-1 until a pitch invasion caused a ten-minute hold up. Newcastle fought back, won the tie 4-3 and were promptly told to replay it by the Football Association. It was staged at Goodison Park and finished 0-0. Newcastle got through at the third attempt, 1-0, and eventually reached the final, where Liverpool beat them 3-0. David Jones stands in disbelief as Newcastle fans are ushered back onto the terraces by the police.

75. There are several well-known faces in this team group, taken in 1969-70. *fourth from the left, back row*, is Paul White, now the club secretary; *second from the right, sitting*, is a fresh-faced John Robertson. The full line up is: *back row, left to right* Serella, Pegram, Collier, White, Piehalnietas, Grimshaw, Bridgett, Harris, McKenzie, Davies, Upton, Styles. *middle row*: Davies (physio), Newton, Winfield, McKinlay, Hill, Chapman, Grummitt, Hindley, Cottam, Brindley Knight (reserve coach), Johnson (youth coach). *third row*: Cavanagh, Moore, Hennesey, Barnwell, O'Kane, Gillies, Richardson, Reece, Hall, Lyons, Hilley, Anderson. *front row*: McCaffrey, Pollock, Buckley, Dilnot, Johnson, Robertson, Cousins.

Champions: The Road to the Title

The forceful header, from the edge of the six yard area, was goal bound before Peter Shilton intuitively launched himself across his line and somehow managed to twist his body, reach up and flick the ball over the bar. This was the save of the season that finally handed the Championship to Nottingham Forest. The stage was Coventry, where Forest won a point and certainly proved one. All season, the question had been whether Forest could pull off a feat that had only been done once before: win the title a season after gaining promotion. When Shilton clawed out the close range effort from Mick Ferguson the answer duly arrived. The Championship belonged to Messrs Clough and Taylor again, with four matches to spare. Such was the strain and effort Forest put into possessing the title, that by the time it was won, most of the players barely had the strength to lift a glass of champagne, let alone celebrate, with the amount of gusto that was going on across the Highfield Road terraces and on the pitch. In the dressing room, Forest sat quietly, congratulating one another on a job well done. A subdued Clough emerged to confess: "Mentally and physically, I'm drained." Asked how he would toast entering the history books as only the second manager to win the Championship with two different clubs (Herbert Chapman achieved it with Huddersfield and Arsenal), he replied "I'll remove my car from the drive at home and sit there with my wife and three children. They were there when I was on the floor and they shared my misery with me. The same people will share my success. I want to sit in an armchair and enjoy the feeling of winning the Championship with my family. I don't want to share it with anyone until I've shared it with them." Later, Clough elaborated: "We were all on our knees. After Coventry, all we wanted to do was get on the coach, go home and fall asleep." Nor was Clough exaggerating when he added: "I didn't believe we'd win the title - until we won it."

76. It may not be breakfast at Tiffany's, but Terry Curran, arriving for £75,000 in a part-exchange deal (Dennis Peacock and Ian Miller going to Doncaster) looks contented enough meeting Alan Hill on his first day as a Forest player.

The master manager had spent much of his time, both privately and publically, refusing to agree that the title was even a possibility; at the same time, those who seriously doubted whether Forest had the calibre and backbone to stay the distance waited expectantly for them to collapse, exhausted, in a heap. In fact, exactly the opposite happened. Forest became stronger, eventually losing only three matches, conceding a meagre 24 goals and, if the truth is told, they never looked susceptible. On a bright August afternoon, they announced themselves emphatically to the rest of the First Division by slaying Everton 3-1 at Goodison Park ("Afterwards, we kept tossing questions at ourselves", smiled Ian Bowyer, "What had we been doing, messing about in the Second Division? This First Division is easy").

Apart from a three goal lesson given to them by Arsenal and the setback of slender defeats at Chelsea and Leeds, the Championship became a realistic proposition from early October when Forest emerged as leaders. No one ever managed to dislodge them. The challenge gained strength and even more credence at Old Trafford, where Manchester United, demolished 4-0, were memorably put through the shredder: "It was a key result," said Clough. A City Ground draw against the formidable Liverpool, pre-season favourites to lift the title, was equally as valuable. Liverpool finally finished in second place, seven points adrift; Manchester City and Everton trailed further behind; and captain, John McGovern, revealed what he believed was the secret behind the success: "Most of us were hungry for success. The hunger grew and the side went from strength to strength. There were these talented players, who would run the legs off anybody - and I mean anybody. There was the fearlessness of youth to try things without worrying about them".

Significantly, of the 16 players used during the season, six had been at Forest when Clough took over; four were bought in his first 18 months and another two arrived in the promotion year. McGovern ("I've bought him to show the others how to play", said Clough) and John O'Hare were shrewdly signed in a £60,000 package deal - £90,000 less than the pair cost Leeds when Clough was manager; £30,000 was all it took to buy Colin Barrett; Frank Clark was picked up on a free transfer when Newcastle inexplicably decided to release him; Peter Withe (£44,000) and Larry Lloyd (£60,000) were typical Clough and Taylor bargains. From the squad Clough inherited came Tony Woodcock, the vastly influential John Robertson, Viv Anderson (who became the first black player to win an England cap), Ian Bowyer, Martin O'Neill and John Middleton. Kenny Burns, Archie Gemmill, Peter Shilton and David Needham arrived between Forest reaching the First Division and ruling it. So the core of the promotion side (Terry Curran was the noticeable absentee) also captured the Championship and then the European Cup (with, of course, the significant addition of Garry Birtles). After promotion, Clough and Taylor wasted no time in supplementing the squad. The Shilton deal was a coup and it put Forest into the record books; no one else had dared pay as much as £270,000 for a goalkeeper (the success of the Shilton move was actually a turning point in the domestic game, dramatically increasing the price for keepers and earning them renewed respect.) The price tag was vindicated time and again by Shilton, who with the combative combination of Lloyd and Burns in front of him saved points where and when it mattered. Burns' performances won him the Footballer of the Year award. The intervention of Clough and Taylor also pointed him towards the 1978 World Cup, where Scotland went to Argentina carrying acute dillusions of grandeur. As the title was being won, Burns assessed the unique Clough-Taylor partnership and pinned its prosperity down to one important factor: "Simplicity". He argued: "The management were just concerned about the basics. They let you get on with your own game. If it wasn't going right, they would soon tell you. That's why Clough and Taylor went together like gin and tonic, lager and lime. The boss might have a go at you, then Peter would come along and say you were in tip-top shape. It made you feel good again."

While appreciating the enormous debt Forest owed to Burns and Shilton in that season, Clough unhesitatingly labels Gemmill as his most significant signing. "We got him for buttons - about £25,000 - and he was the best pro we had on our books. Better than Shilton. Better than Burns. His approach, his attitude and his all-round know how were precious. When Burnsy first arrived, he didn't know what day it was. On the morning I signed him, I was judging a sweet pea competition - Burnsy thought you put them on your plate for Sunday lunch. As for Shilts, it tends to be forgotten that he hadn't won a solitary thing in his career before he came here. I signed him shortly after seeing him play for Stoke at Mansfield ... hardly the big time, was it? The pair of them didn't give me a scrap of trouble. They were both like choir boys off the pitch and played like geniuses on it. Others were dreadfully under-rated - except at this club - like Lloyd, Clark and McGovern."

Clough had not the slightest trepidation about tackling the First Division. He felt that, if nothing else, Forest could hold their own. Unlikely as it may seem, he did have to conquer an element of self-doubt before he got there, after the traumas of Brighton and Leeds. He explained it for the first time on the tenth anniversary of lifting the Championship. "There's always a bit of self doubt about, even for a big head like me. To the outside world, it seemed as if I'd nose-dived from being the best manager in the Football League to scratching around in the Third Division when I went from Derby to Brighton. And then Leeds was a disaster. So getting promotion restored my credibility, not only to one or two people within the game, but mostly to myself. After that, I wasn't remotely worried. But I honestly didn't think we'd win the title at the start of that season and it wasn't until we'd faced most sides twice that I realised we had a chance. From then on, the belief began to grow."

77. Viv Anderson, the first black player to win a full England cap, clearly resists the temptation to fall asleep in 1976.

How different things might have been. On Clough's admission, Forest "could have been relegated in my first season. I nearly lost my first six matches and the job was tougher than I expected." His evaluation of the club was brutal and candid: "The place had its priorities wrong. Some of the squad had no fire, no determination and I got the impression that a few of them didn't care."

In his first season, Forest completed an unexpected piece of FA Cup giant killing by beating Tottenham, yet finished sixteenth in the table - two places below Notts County and only five points from relegation. In the second year, he hoisted them to 8th place. In 1977, promotion arrived (as had Taylor 10 months earlier), with Wolves kindly propping the door ajar by beating Bolton and letting Forest cling to third place on an afternoon when the entire squad was airborne, en-route to Majorca for a summer break. The bookmakers would have offered generous odds on Forest capturing the First Division Championship at any time, let alone within a year of those Spanish celebrations. Along with the title, Forest chalked up a quite incredible run of games without defeat, stretching from 26 November 1977 to 9 December 1978 - then the equivalent of an entire season. It started unspectacularly with a goalless draw at West Bromwich Albion and ended at Liverpool, where Forest were severely weakened by injuries. Clough was so proud of the achievement that he had his own silver salver struck detailing every game. "We're in the record books - and we'll stay there for ever more," he said. He has not been proved wrong yet.

The following season, Forest were second, then fifth and seventh before slipping below half way in the table, the prelude to a comeback that saw them climb to third place in 1984 and then again in 1988. The Championship, it must be said, still remains the primary objective for Clough, ahead of any other piece of silverware. "I've maintained all along that any reasonable side can win a Cup if the breaks go for them. The Championship is different altogether. It's always meant more to me than anything - even the European Cup - because it's the supreme and ultimate test. The fact our League is the toughest in the world makes it even more prestigious. I'm not kidding when I say I'd swop a Championship for any trophy you cared to name. I got more pleasure out of the two titles at Derby and Forest than all the other things I've achieved in this game. That's why I want to get another one under my belt before I retire - that, by the way, will be in about two hundred years time."

78. Clough snaps up John McGovern (left) and John O'Hare from his former club, Leeds.

79. The first trophy. Forest beat Orient 5-1 on aggregate to capture the Anglo Scottish Cup, the prelude to an 18 month trophy blitz. John McGovern collects a trophy that manager Brian Clough insists was crucial. "The people who said the Cup was a nothing event were absolutely crackers. It was something to us, to the club and to the players. It provided us with a bit of silverware and those players who hadn't won anything in their professional careers got a medal. We tasted the champagne - and we liked it."

80. The squad Clough inherited, plus a few additions, a few months after his arrival: *back row, left to right*: Tony Woodcock, Jimmy McCann, Glyn Saunders, Ian Miller, Viv Anderson, John Robertson, David Gill: *second row:* Alan Hill, Bert Bowery, Paul Richardson, Ian Bowyer, Lian O'Kane, Dennis Peacock, John Middleton, Peter Wells, Martin O'Neill, Jimmy McIntosh, David Dall, John Sheridan, Peter Blakey, Brian Clough. *third row*: Jimmy Gordon, John McGovern, David Jones, John O'Hare, Barry Butlin, Sammy Chapman, George Lyall, Frank Clark, John Cottam. *front row*: Stephen Elliott, Steve Bissell, Bryan Gunn, John Mee, John Powell, Vince Bedford, Cieran McCurry,

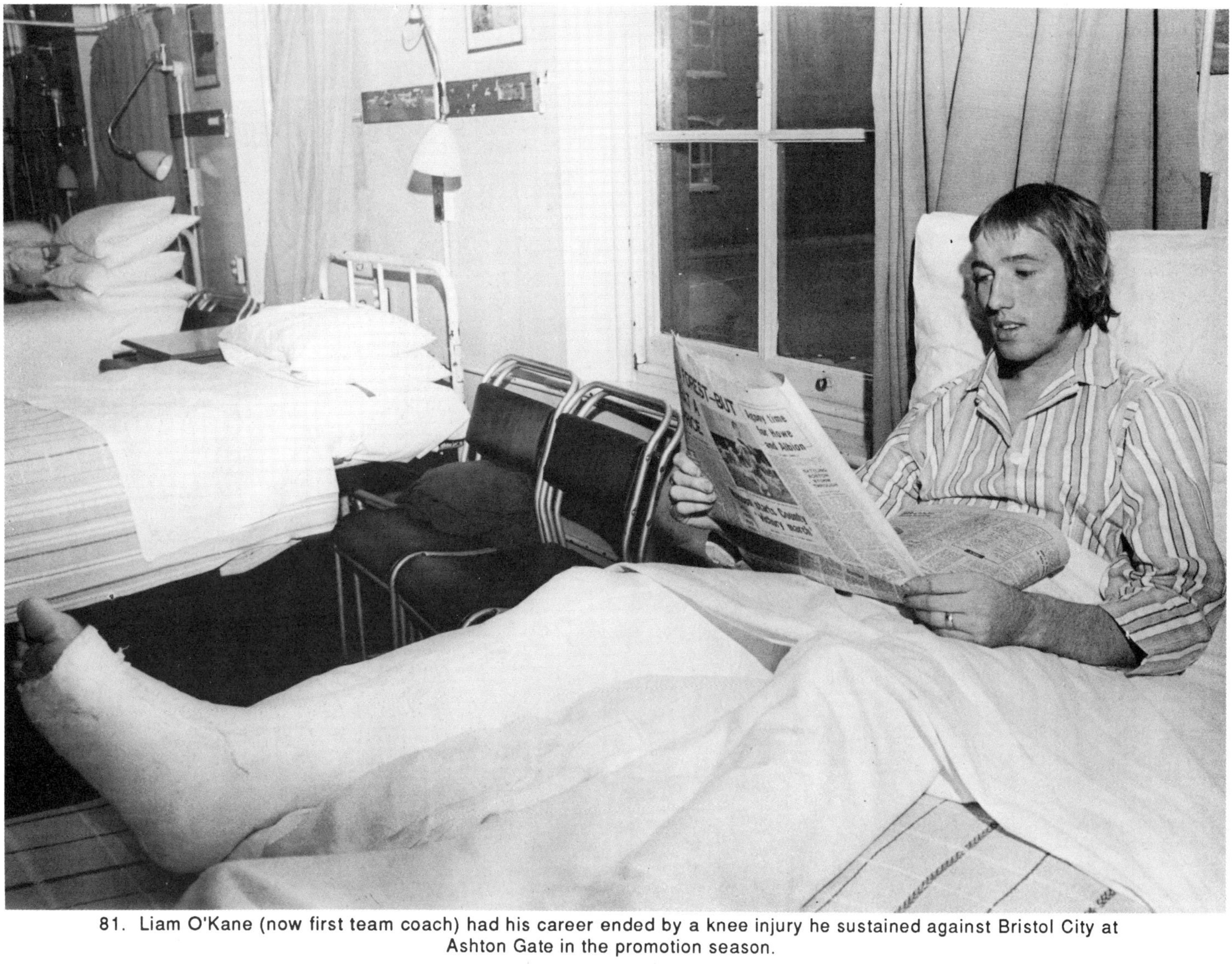

81. Liam O'Kane (now first team coach) had his career ended by a knee injury he sustained against Bristol City at Ashton Gate in the promotion season.

82. The squad before the start of the 1977-78 season. *back row, left to right:* Jimmy Gordon, Bryan Gunn, Martin O'Neill, Ian Bowyer, Peter Withe, Viv Anderson, John Middleton, Garry Birtles, Barry Butlin,Colin Barrett, Kenny Burns, Brian Clough. *front row:* Larry Lloyd, Sean Hastlegrave, Frank Clark, John McGovern, John Robertson, Terry Curran, Tony Woodcock.

83. "We got Archie Gemmill for buttons", said Clough. "And he was the best pro we had on the books." Gemmill signs for Forest alongside John Middleton (who went to Derby in an exchange deal), Derby boss Tommy Docherty and Stuart Webb.

84. Tony Woodcock winning the Forest Player of the Year award, presented by boss Brian Clough. He was soon to depart to Cologne. UEFA regulations set the size of the fee at £650,000.

85. Forest rewrote the record book by signing Peter Shilton shortly after the start of the Championship season. The £300,000 transfer of Shilton was the highest fee paid for a goalkeeper.

86. It's ours. John McGovern (*centre*), Kenny Burns (*left*) and Peter Shilton proudly parade the Championship trophy.

87. Burns goes on a lap of honour with his partner Larry Lloyd.

88. The team on the balcony of the Council House.

89. Side by side: Clough and Taylor. The proud possessors of another League title.

90. The Whole World in our Hands. When Forest weren't breaking records, the squad made them. It actually reached the charts.

91, 92 & 93. *above*: Jimmy Gordon departed from Leeds alongside Clough. When the master manager moved to the City Ground, Clough made him his first signing - snapping him up from Rolls Royce in Derby, where the ebullient Gordon had been working since the 44 day disaster at Elland Road. Gordon with George Lyall *(centre)* and Barry Butlin on the field. *right*: Doing a bit of polishing off with his domestic and European trophies. *below*: The achievement of going 42 League games without defeat was recognised bythe Football League. A plaque was presented by the then League President Jack Dunnett to Messrs Clough, Taylor and chairman Stuart Dryden *(extreme left)*.

94-95. *above:* Peter Shilton made the save of the season to seal the Championship for Forest in 1977-78. He denied Coventry striker Mick Ferguson as Forest held Coventry to a 0-0 draw at Highfield Road. *below:* Shilton keeps out Ferguson again in the same match.

96 & 97. *above*: Martin O'Neill drives in a shot during the goalless game. *below*: The day the title was won: Kenny Burns and John O'Hare *(extreme left)* walk off the pitch at Highfield Road after the draw with Coventry confirms Forest as Champions.

98. Smiles, but no champagne. Brian Clough, chairman Brian Appleby, Peter Taylor and Stuart Dryden, photographed after the title was all but assured. By then, Forest needed only one point to take the Championship. But when Clough was asked whether the celebrations were about to start, he insisted: "What, for the League Cup?"

99. Burns crowns the year by winning the Footballer of the Year award at the Cafe Royal.

	P	W	D	L	F	A	W	D	L	F	A	Pts
Nottingham F	42	15	6	0	37	8	10	8	3	32	16	64
Liverpool	42	15	4	2	37	11	9	5	7	28	23	57
Everton	42	14	4	3	47	22	8	7	6	29	23	55
Manchester C	42	14	4	3	46	21	6	8	7	28	30	52
Arsenal	42	14	5	2	38	12	7	5	9	22	25	52
WBA	42	13	5	3	35	18	5	9	7	27	35	50
Coventry C	42	13	5	3	48	23	5	7	9	27	39	48
Aston Villa	42	11	4	6	33	18	7	6	8	24	24	46
Leeds U	42	12	4	5	39	21	6	6	9	24	32	46
Manchester U	42	9	6	6	32	23	7	4	10	35	40	42
Birmingham C	42	8	5	8	32	30	8	4	9	23	30	41
Derby Co	42	10	7	4	37	24	4	6	11	17	35	41
Norwich C	42	10	8	3	28	20	1	10	10	24	46	40
Middlesbrough	42	8	8	5	25	19	4	7	10	17	35	39
Wolverhampton W	42	7	8	6	30	27	5	4	12	21	37	36
Chelsea	42	7	11	3	28	20	4	3	14	18	49	36
Bristol C	42	9	6	6	37	26	2	7	12	12	27	35
Ipswich T	42	10	5	6	32	24	1	8	12	15	37	35
OPR	42	8	8	5	27	26	1	7	13	20	38	33
West Ham U	42	8	6	7	31	28	4	2	15	21	41	32
Newcastle U	42	4	6	11	26	37	2	4	15	16	41	22
Leicester C	42	4	7	10	16	32	1	5	15	10	38	22

Kings of Europe

The trail towards the first European Cup was begun by a striker bought for virtually nothing and finished by another who cost one million pounds. The second Euoropean Cup was won as much in a bleak car park in East Berlin as it was on a balmy night in the palatial Bernabeu Stadium. Scarcely can more diverse routes have led to the summit of Europe in successive seasons. That Nottingham Forest were parading the bulbous trophy around the opulent Olympic Stadium in Munich only two years after climbing out of the Second Division was an improbable and remarkable achievement. Along the way, the apprentices of Europe won a domestic affair against Liverpool, overcame the Greeks of AEK Athens, Grasshoppers of Zurich and then provided one of the more striking comebacks in the history of the competition to defeat the West Germans, Cologne.

Garry Birtles was still such a relatively unkown figure in Nottingham, let alone to the First Division - he had made only two League appearances, one of them in midfield - that Liverpool barely recognised him. After Birtles set Forest in motion towards Munich - making the breakthrough with his first ever goal - he made sure the then European Champions would never forget him. Nine months later, Trevor Francis arrived with split second punctuality at the far post to steer in his header and beat the dour, unimaginative Swedes, Malmo. By then Birtles was an established figure. How rapidly life changed for him. He was nearly 21 and laying carpets for a living when Forest signed him from Long Eaton United, of the Midland League, for £2,000 in March 1977. In scoring the first goal against Liverpool and contributing a primary role in creating the second to seal a 2-0 win, Birtles all but established himself overnight. "I kept remembering the manager telling me to get into the box," he said. "Tony Woodcock did all the spadework for my goal. There was the ball at my feet. I thought 'Keep your

101. How it all began. The road to the first European Cup win. The then unknown Garry Birtles puts Forest ahead against Liverpool at the City Ground.

head and slot it in'. I was pleased about the way I stayed calm." Forest mastered the masters again at Anfield, holding them to a goalless draw, and Birtles gave a repeat performance in the next round in the intimidating caldron of Athens, where Forest won 2-1 before dismantling AEK 5-1 in an embarrassingly easy return leg. Grasshoppers, another outfit with limitations, suffered identical treatment, losing 4-1 at the City Ground before eking out a 1-1 draw in Switzerland. Enter Cologne for an epic semi-final in which Forest staged an unforgettable escape act. Walking the high wire, Forest leaked two straightforward goals inside nineteen minutes, fought back to lead after an hour, and were finally held to a 3-3 draw on a ploughed field of a pitch. Cologne went home to book hotel accommodation in Munich. Ian Bowyer, stooping to head in the second leg winner from relatively close range forced overnight cancellations.

It was a tactical triumph that also proved Forest were capable of winning a test of raw nerves. No one outside Nottingham backed them and the versatile Bowyer described his goal as "the most important I ever scored for the club". He won the headlines, but not a place in the League game which immediately followed. Trevor Francis, who sat, cup-tied in the stand in Cologne, took his place. In spite of this the unfashionable, defence-minded Malmo (almost as unlikely finalists as Forest) made the final such a soporific occasion - chances were few and far between and action was strictly rationed - Francis at least saw to it that justice was done. Forest, 1-0 winners, lived up to their label as favourites. Francis' impeccable finish shortly before half time was matched by the precision of the cross that created the opening, a ball stroked in with his left foot by John Robertson.

How fitting that the key figure of Robertson, the subtle architect of so much at the City Ground, and described as "without a doubt, the best player in Europe" by John McGovern, should retain the European Cup exactly a year later when Forest, this time the underdogs, out-fought and out-manoeuvred Hamburg and the ubiquitous Kevin Keegan. Francis was in plaster after tearing his Achilles tendon a month before Madrid. The legacy he left came on a two-overcoat night in the quarter-final acted out behind the Berlin Wall. Not only was the temperature as low as minus three, Forest also happened to be a goal behind from the first leg and had disappointingly lost the League Cup final to Wolves only four days earlier. In contrast, Dynamo Berlin prepared for the tie by winning a League match 10-0. A funeral in Berlin for Forest was widely anticipated.

It was a 100 yard walk across a car park from

102. After Liverpool, Forest were drawn against AEK Athens. The Greeks were demolished 7-2 on aggregate (5-1 at the City Ground). Garry Birtles delivers the killer blow in Athens. grabbing the second goal.

the dressing room to the pitch: Enough time for Peter Taylor to decide in his own mind that Forest were going to defy the odds: "It was the longest walk out to a pitch I have ever experienced. And if there had been a betting shop on the way, I'd have backed us to pull it off without the slightest hesitation. Dynamo were so frightened that most of them looked like zombies. I knew they'd freeze." The Taylor calculation was right. Francis scored twice in a 3-1 win and Dynamo became another scalp on the campaign trail. Wins were notched up against the modest Oester Vaxjo from Sweden (3-1 on aggregate), the Romanians Arges Pitesti (4-1) and the more formidable Ajax (2-1) in the semi-finals, including a particularly tense second leg in Amsterdam.

So to Spain. Apart from Robertson's goal early in the first half - "it was always going away from the keeper and I could see where it would finish up immediately" - that denied Keegan and Hamburg, the final itself emphasised the classic defending skills of the indefatigable Kenny Burns and the supreme quality of Peter Shilton, time and again making classic saves. Robertson, admitting that "when I was a kid, I thought the European Cup was for Puskas, Di Stefano and legends like that," was as accurate with his post-match assessment as his decisive, low shot. "We couldn't have done a better job in a professional sort of way." Forest spent most of the time defending. "We didn't think we could attack Hamburg because, technically, the side was good on the ball. It was like playing Liverpool; no matter what, you always know they'll have 60-65 per cent of the ball. If you make them play square and across, there's not going to be much danger." Keegan went deeper, vainly attempting to orchestrate from the half way line instead of in and around the area where he was most effective; and Forest, it ought to be stressed, might have stretched the lead Robertson gave them if Birtles had not been so exhausted as to slip over when he attempted a long, lone run.

103. Off guard in Athens in 1979.

It was entirely predictable that Forest should find themselves strongly backed for a European Cup hat-trick. Those ambitions were killed off at the first hurdle by the Bulgarian army team CSKA Sofia five months later. Robertson, crucially, hit a post from long range in the first leg, a stroke of ill-luck that denied them an important away goal. But the morning after the night before - when Forest failed to win on their own pitch - Brian Clough acted as champagne waiter to a posse of more than a dozen journalists. As the last bottle was being opened, Clough vanished then reappeared a minute later carrying the European Cup. "Come on lads, let's have our picture taken alongside this thing. It might never come back, so take the chance while it's here." The photograph still stands on the mantlepiece of his office.

As European Cup holders, Forest were still entitled to another two continental missions, the first to defend the Super Cup (captured twelve months earlier by beating Barcelona) and an appearance in the World Club Championship final by travelling to Tokyo, where the South Americans, Nacional, awaited them. Valencia narrowly beat them in the Super Cup; the side from Uruguay won 1-0 in the Olympic Stadium, despite being inferior on a hard, uneven surface shorn almost completely of grass. Japan had been nothing more than a stop-over to Forest; 32 hours flying time in four days, squeezed in between a League game and an FA Cup-tie. Nacional had been camped in Tokyo for almost a fortnight.

It was another three years, post-CSKA, before the door to Europe opened invitingly again - this time to the UEFA Cup - and how desperately close Forest, with a remodelled team, came to capitalising on it. After dismissing East Germans, Vorwarts, and the Dutch, PSV Eindhoven, the third round draw paired them in a Battle of Britain against Celtic; goalless on a frost bound pitch at the City Ground, a win at cavernous Parkhead when Celtic (a la Cologne) were expected to remove them. The semi-final with Anderlecht - after Sturm Graz of Austria were beaten - was swathed in controversey. Forest, two goals ahead from the first leg, were behind 3-0 when Paul Hart headed what appeared to be a perfectly legitimate goal in the last minute that would have taken them through on the away goals rule. Shepherd over the line by Bowyer, the ball went through a thicket of bodies, only to be disallowed by the referee. They qualified again after finishing third in the First Division and promptly went out to Bruges of Belgium.

Even in the absence of European competition - owing to UEFA's ban - there is one consolation for Forest. The prestige of being former European Cup holders is significant even now. "We liked Europe. We treated it like a holiday, in the sense that it was a break from the demands of the League," said Clough. "And we've still done what others will only achieve in their dreams. Our name is on the trophy and no one will ever scratch it off. That's really something for Nottingham to be proud of. When I first came to the club, the biggest thrill around the place - not for me - was beating Notts County to win the County Cup or finishing above them in the table. It was the be all and end all."

"I think things have changed."

EUROPEAN CUP: 1978-79

First round:	Forest 2 (Birtles, Barrett) Liverpool 0
Second leg:	Liverpool 0, Forest 0
Second round:	AEK Athens 1, Forest 2 (McGovern, Birtles)
Second leg:	Forest 5, (Birtles 2 Needham,Woodcock Anderson), AEK Athens 1
Quarter finals:	Forest 4,(Birtles, Robertson penalty Gemmill,Lloyd, Grasshoppers 1
Second leg:	Grasshoppers 1, Forest 1 (O'Neill)
Semi finals:	Forest 3, (Birtles, Bowyer, Robertson), Cologne 3
Second leg:	Cologne 0, Forest 1 (Bowyer)
FINAL:	(Munich) Forest 1, Malmo 0 (Francis)

EUROPEAN CUP: 1979-80

First round:	Forest 2, (Bowyer 2), Oesters Vaxjo 0
Second leg:	Oesters Vaxjo 1, Forest 1 (Woodcock)
Second round:	Forest 2 (Woodcock,Birtles), Arges Pitesti
Second leg:	Arges Pitesti 1, Forest 2 (Bowyer, Birtles)
Quarter finals:	Forest 0, Dynamo Berlin 1
Second leg:	Dynamo Berlin 1, Forest 3 (Francis 2, Robertson)
Semi final:	Forest 2 (Francis,Robertson penalty),Ajax
Second leg:	Ajax 1, Forest 0
FINAL:	(Madrid) Forest 1 (Robertson), Hamburg 0

104. In the second leg against AEK, Viv Anderson staked his claim for goal of the season. The England defender is not only out of the picture - he was out of the penalty area as well.

V-VI. Trevor Francis scores the winning goal in the 1979 European Cup final against Malmo.
below: John McGovern and Larry Loyd with the trophy.

VII. Super Cup winners in Barcelona.

105. Cologne keeper Schumacher beats out an effort from Ian Bowyer.

106. John Robertson in the unlikely role of 'Tommy Lawton', with a diving headed goal in the first leg against Cologne.

107. Defender Colin Barrett turns attacker as he tries, unsuccessfully, to force his way past the Cologne defence and Schumacher.

108. The 1979 semi final against Cologne was an epic affair played on a ploughed field of a pitch. Martin O'Neill battles as much against the mud as he does the white-shirted Cologne defence. The scoreboard tells the story. The number 14, up in lights, belonged to a Japanese player Okudera, a second half substitute. It provoked predictable national newspaper headlines the following morning 'FOREST SUNK BY JAP SUB'.

109. The odds were stacked against them. No one-outside Nottingham - backed Forest to beat Cologne in the vast Mungesdorf Stadium after the 3-3 draw at the City Ground. But in the 65th minute, Ian Bowyer headed the goal that sealed an improbable win. His reward? Bowyer was dropped 72 hours later to make way fro Trevor Francis in the First Division.

110. The goalscorer and the goalkeeper. Ian Bowyer and Peter Shilton after Forest had out-witted Cologne.

111. Tony Woodcock proves he's a high flier in the Olympic Stadium, Munich.

112. Woodcock fires in a shot from the edge of the Malmo penalty area.

113. Tony Woodcock is out-numbered three to one by the Swedes. So defence-minded Malmo made the 1979 final a soporific affair.

114. On the overlap, Viv Anderson pushes over a cross after escaping from the drag-net defence of Malmo.

115. Garry Birtles and Tony Woodcock *(centre)* are merely by-standers; Jan Moller is beaten by a shot from John McGovern *(out of the picture)* - the effort drifts off target.

116. The £1m goal. John Robertson gets to the by-line; Trevor Francis meets his cross with split second punctuality at the far post. Forest 1, Malmo 0. It was Francis' first game in Europe since his seven figure transfer from Birmingham City.

117. Smiles of success. Robertson with Tony Woodcock *(left)*.

118. Even Fred Astair never wore a top hat like this: Larry Lloyd lets the European Cup win over Malmo go to his head.

119. Champions: *back row, left to right*: Anderson, Shilton, Woods, McGovern, Bowyer, Needham, Francis, Clark, O'Hare *(hidden)*, Gordon. *front row*: Lloyd, Robertson, Woodcock, Burns, Birtles. There was no Martin O'Neill or Archie Gemmill - both were injured.

120 & 121. The man who broke the Berlin Wall. Trevor Francis was asked by Brian Clough before the tie against Dynamo Berlin, where he wanted to play. "Up front" was the instant reply. It paid off. Forest, a goal behind from the first leg in the quarter finals of the 1980 European Cup, won the return 3-1. Francis scored twice.

122. The Dutch were totally baffled when Nottingham Forest supporters began wearing T-shirts with the slogan: "We'll wipe the floor with Ajax". The cleaning product apparently didn't exist in Holland. Anyhow, Forest were as good as their word, edging them out 2-1 on aggregate in the semi final. Trevor Francis laid the foundations with this close range effort.

123. The team and officials leave for the return leg against Ajax of Amsterdam.

124. *left:* Apart from having to beat Peter Shilton, Hamburg also had to get past the indomitable Kenny Burns.

125. *right:* Felix Magath is frustrated by this superb Shilton save from a free kick.

126. *below:* The European Cup could not be in safer hands. The unbeatable Peter Shilton.

127. John Robertson was better known for creating goals than scoring them (despite the fact he claimed his fair share, particularly penalties). His European Cup winner in Madrid was also driven in with his right foot. Ian Bowyer stands aside as Robertson, going past Kaltz, plays a one-two with Garry Birtles and drills in his 20 yard shot after 21 minutes. "I can remember shouting 'goal' to myself before the ball even hit the net", he said.

128. Robertson, McGovern and Bowyer watch the drive find its target.

129. The 1980 final was compensation for Martin O'Neill, who missed Munich suffering from fitness problems. Madrid was no night to remember for the unfortunate Kevin Keegan (right). The deeper he went, the easier it became for Forest. The Hamburg number ten is Felix Magath.

130. Gary Mills made an appearance in Europe as a 16 year old. By the time the 1980 European Cup final arrived, he was at least able to vote.

131. Gary Mills and Viv Anderson on the customary lap of honour around the Bernabeu Stadium, Madrid.

VIII & IX. Ian Wallace *(above)* and Martin O'Neill in action against Nacional during the World Club Championship in Tokyo.

X. Garry Birtles.

XI. John McGovern and Martin O'Neill.

XII. Trevor Francis scores against Dynamo Berlin in the European Cup.

XIII. Forest celebrate John Robertson's winning goal in the 1980 European Cup Final.

XIV. Kenny Burns, with the European Cup, 1980.

132. The European Cup winners 1980: *back row, left to right*: Mills, Bowyer, Birtles, O'Hare, Robertson. *middle row*: Gordon, Gunn, Needham, Shilton, Montgomery, Lloyd, O'Neill, Burns. *front row*: Francis, McGovern, Taylor, Clough, Geoffrey Macpherson (chairman), Gray, Anderson.

133 & 134. *above*: Larry Lloyd parading the European Cup and his own natty head gear on the balcony of the Council House in 1980. *below*: The ecstasy of a city with a Euro-beating team. Forest come home in 1979.

135-136. *above:* The European Cup wins opened the door to the Super Cup. Forest won their first one against Barcelona and lost the second to Valencia. In the opulent Nou Camp Stadium, Kenny Burns' classic header broke the heart of Barcelona. *below:* Super Reds win the Super Cup. Some of them - like Peter Shilton and John Robertson - don't look particularly pleased about it. The line up is *back row, left to right:* O'Neill, Lloyd, Anderson, Bowles, George, Needham, a stone-faced Shilton. *front row:* Gray, McGovern, Burns, Birtles, Robertson.

137 & 138. Martin O'Neill is crowded into a three-cornered fight for the ball and Ian Wallace cannot find a way through, either.Volatile Valencia - including Argentina's World Cup winner Mario Kempes - levered the Super Cup out of Forest's grasp, winning on away goals after the tie finished 2-2 on aggregate. The second leg in Spain was slightly scarred by a few injudicious tackles from Valencia. Suffice to say, there was no love lost in the Luis Casanova Stadium.

.9. The Football League refused Forest
·rmission to cancel a League game at
anchester City and the Football Association
ould not let them re-schedule an FA Cup tie
ainst Bristol City. So Forest squeezed in
marathon haul to Tokyo and back for the
orld Club Championship - the trip was four
ys long - between those two games. The
outh Americans, Nacional, of Uruguay, had
ready been in Japan for more than a week
d a half. Forest lost 1-0 to a goal from
ctorino (who also won a car from the
onsors, Toyota, for being man of the
atch) despite being vastly more
pressive. The team was: Shilton,
nderson Gray (F), Ponte (Ward), Lloyd,
rns, O'Neill, Wallace, Francis, Gray (S),
obertson. At least Brian Clough and Peter
aylor did get their hands on the trophy,
beit at a press conference in London to
omote the match.

40. The striker who took it away from them - Victorino scores the only goal after ten minutes.

141-142. *above:* Ian Wallace tries to escape the attention of two Nacional defenders in the Olympic Stadium, Tokyo. His striking partner is Trevor Francis. *below:* Viv Anderson climbs above Brandts to clear a PSV Eindhoven attack as Paul Hart, Ian Wallace, Hans Van Breukelen and Colin Todd stand poised for action.

143. The all-British third round UEFA Cup tie in 1984 - Forest against Celtic - produced a sell-out at the City Ground. The pitch was so hard that Torvill and Dean could have skated on it. Celtic eked out a goalless draw, closing down Forest, as Peter Davenport (surrounded by three defenders) soon found out.

144. Life was no easier for his partner, Ian Wallace, after he forced a brave save from Celtic 'keeper Pat Bonner.

145. Skipper Danny McGrain also has the odd word of advice for his fellow countryman.

146. Steve Hodge breaks the deadlock. Colin Walsh was the other scorer.

147. Hodge's upraised finger gives the Scots a cricket-type verdict "You're out".

148. The dressing room dance: Forest after whipping Celtic 2-1 at Parkhead. *back row, left to right*: Sutton, Walker, Van Breukelen, Sinclair, O'Kane, Hill, Verity. *middle row*: Gunn, Smalley, Shaw, Fenton, Longhurst. *front row*: Davenport, Murray, Birtles, Wigley, Swain, Walsh, Hodge, Clough, Fairclough, Hart, Anderson.

149 & 150. *above*: Forest kept their word about tying Celtic in knots. Brian Clough, Viv Anderson and Colin Walsh on board a replica of the Golden Hind, anchored on the West coast of Scotland. It wasn't the only piece of typical Clough preparation, either. Forest stayed at Troon and tested themselves on the championship golf course and, on the way from the airport to the hotel, Clough took his players into a pub owned by Celtic manager David Hay. "We'll all have a drink - and put it on David's bill". said Clough. The bemused barman did as he was told. *right*: When Brian Clough thrust his fist into the bark of a tree during the build up to the UEFA quarter final against Sturm Graz - Forest stayed in a mountain resort, away from the press and supporters - the team stared at him in disbelief. "It's called a Punch Tree". said Clough. "The bark is so soft, its like a sponge." He asked the players to smuggle it back to Nottingham for his garden.

151. Captain Ian Bowyer was an inspirational figure as Forest's UEFA Cup tie in Graz went into extra time.

152. Celebrating his birthday in Graz (1984). The cake was ordered and delivered by the journalists on the UEFA Cup trip.

153 & 154. *above*: Steve Hodge claims his first goal in the first leg of the UEFA Cup semi final against the Belgians, from a Steve Wigley cross. *below*: He heads in number two.

155-156. Instead of being part of the 1984 UEFA Cup final, Brian Clough had to assume a secondary role, as television commentator for ITV; all because of one incident in the last minute of the semi-final against Anderlecht. Forest won the first leg 2-0 and lost the second 3-0 (Anderlecht were given a penalty that the TV highlights proved was dubious to say the least). *above right:* Paul Hart climbs above defender Michel de Groote. As the minutes drained away, Forest had what seemed to be a perfectly legitimate goal disallowed by Spanish referee Guruceta Muro that would have taken them through to meet Tottenham on the away goals rule. *right:* The ball goes into the net and referee Muro looks on impassively.

157. Ian Bowyer turns to celebrate - the referee signals a free kick.

XV. John Robertson.

XVI. Stuart Pearce.

XVII. Steve Sutton.

XVIII. Des Walker.

XIX. Gary Crosby.

XX. Terry Wilson.

Wembley Way

158. On Wembley Way. It took Brian Clough thirteen years in management before he reached his first major Wembley final, the 1978 League Cup final. He is pictured here with Liverpool manager Bob Paisley.

159. Chris Woods frustrated Liverpool for 120 minutes at Wembley and another 90 at Old Trafford. This save from Terry McDermott (with Viv Anderson left sprawling on the floor) was typical of his mature performance. Kenny Burns gives moral support from inside the six yard area.

160. Chris Woods was beaten once at Wembley - and it didn't count. Terry McDermott *(out of picture)* drives in a low shot beyond Woods' despairing dive only to discover Kenny Dalglish had drifted offside. Kenny Burns and Larry Lloyd can hardly bear to watch. Frank Clark, on his knees, takes a rather more phlegmatic view of affairs. The Liverpool player is Ian Callaghan.

161. Peter Withe fails to get past full back Phil Neal at Wembley.

162. Ray Kennedy unable to find a way past Viv Anderson and Martin O'Neill inside the Forest area.

163. John O'Hare fights for possession with Kennedy in the replay.

164. The penalty Liverpool still argue about. Was John O'Hare in or outside the area when he was brought down by Phil Thompson? The referee, Pat Partridge, didn't hesitate to give Forest the penalty. Thompson argued: "I tripped him outside the box".

165. John Robertson slides his penalty home in front of a captive audience *from left to right*: Terry McDermott, Peter Withe, Jimmy Case, John O'Hare and Tommy Smith. Forest 1, Liverpool 0.

166. The winning salute. *from left to right:* John O'Hare, Tony Woodcock, Martin O'Neill, Kenny Burns, John Robertson and Larry Lloyd on a lap of honour at Old Trafford.

167. Larry Lloyd *(left)* and Frank Clark celebrate the win over Liverpool at Old Trafford.

168. Peter Taylor, daughter Wendy, son Philip and wife Lilian, with the League Cup. "They deserve to share in it all because they have been as much a part of it as me", said the Forest assistant manager.

169. The Football League were frustratingly intransigent when Forest asked for a special dispensation so that both Brian Clough and Peter Taylor could lead the players out at Wembley before the League Cup final against Liverpool. The League, fearing a precedent, turned them down. Clough lead the players out in 1978; Taylor (followed by John McGovern, Peter Shilton, Colin Barrett and Larry Lloyd) finally got his chance when Forest returned twelve months later. Jimmy Gordon was given the honour the following season against Wolves.

170. The camera clearly can lie. This looks certain to be another goal for Garry Birtles *(out of picture)*. But Nick Holmes (left) actually scooped the ball clear after it rolled across the line, just when Tony Woodcock was about to launch the celebrations.

171-172. *above:* Garry Birtles suddenly knows what it's like to be in demand after scoring the equaliser against Southampton. The players playing tribute to him are John Robertson (*left*) and Tony Woodcock. Forest, a goal down at half-time, finally won the trophy at a relative canter. *above right:* Chris Nicholl (now the Southampton manager) is on his knees after Birtles pushes the ball past Terry Gennoe for his second goal. It was Birtles' debut season as a first teamer.

173. The League Cup belongs to Nottingham Forest again after Southampton are beaten 3-2. It's especially significant for Archie Gemmill *(extreme left)*, Peter Shilton, Colin Barrett *(hidden)* and David Needham *(centre)*, all of whom missed the win over Liverpool.

174. As captain of Wolves, Emlyn Hughes *(centre)* gained his revenge on Forest for Liverpool's 1978 League Cup defeat. He shepherds the ball back to goalkeeper Paul Bradshaw before Martin O'Neill *(left)*, Ian Bowyer and Garry Birtles *(extreme right)* can fasten onto the chance. The other Wolves defender is George Berry.

175. Martin O'Neill fires a free kick into the Wolves wall.

176. So near and yet so far. Frank Gray agonisingly watches the ball roll wide as he stumbles over Paul Bradshaw and defender George Berry.

177. That winning feeling for Wolves - Paul Bradshaw, revealing as much relief as satisfaction.

178. No lap of honour this time - and no hat trick, either - after being beaten 1-0 by Wolves; merely a feeling of what might have been for John Robertson, Martin O'Neill, David Needham and captain John McGovern.

179. Martin O'Neill still holds the distinction of being the club's most capped player. He won 34 caps (64 in all) for Northern Ireland. O'Neill superbly finishes inside the area for his second goal before Brian Talbot *(left)* can close him down.

180. O'Neill skillfully places his shot beyond Paul Cooper. The Ipswich defenders are Russell Osman and Brian Talbot.

181. Tony Woodcock takes a divot out of the immaculate Wembley pitch driving in a shot blocked by Russell Osman *(left)*. John Wark provides the extra cover.

182. John McGovern and Archie Gemmill hold aloft the Charity Shield after their emphatic 5-0 win over Ipswich at the beginning of the 1978-79 season.

Saturday's Men

183. The first £1m man in British history took his bow in front of less than 50 supporters and a dog. The stage was a windswept Grove Farm; the opposition were Notts County. Enter Trevor Francis. The sight of Francis incongruously plying his trade in the Midland Intermediate League, less than 24 hours after signing his way into the Guinness Book of Records, was not as completely bizarre as it seemed. The previous day, as Francis answered questions at a press conference so congested that it almost matched the average home gate, he was invariably asked when he would make his debut. "When I pick him", interjected Brian Clough, before Francis could draw breath. The decision had already been made. There was a reason for it, too. Francis had played only one match in the previous five weeks in a season blighted by bad weather. So began Francis' eventful stay at the City Ground and, while breaking new ground, it was never regarded as a gamble by Clough. "If we decided to sell him we'll get our money back overnight". Clough was right. Manchester City paid in excess of £1m for him two and a half years later. A succession of injuries shrouded Francis' stint at Forest. *right*: Francis is helped off the pitch by Ron Fenton and Tony Verity.

184. Walking off after playing his first match for nearly eight months - he had torn his Achilles tendon - in the second leg of the Super Cup in Valencia.

XXI. Nigel Clough.

XXII. The FA Cup semi final squad, 1988.

185. Not even the lira of Pisa - a £1.5m bid - could persuade Nottingham Forest to sell Nigel Clough. This is how his goal scoring feats started, with a diving header against Watford in May 1985.

186. A classic header by Nigel Clough beats Peter Shilton.

187-189. *above:* This is your captain speaking . . . if you think Stuart Pearce's salute hardly meets captain's standard, what about Brian Clough's thumbs up? The Forest manager has just appointed Pearce skipper. Also pictured is assistant manager Ron Fenton. *right:* Justin Fashanu was banned from the training ground before taking the short trip to Notts County for £125,000 just 32 League appearances and three goals later. *below:* Ian Wallace puts away this horizontal header against Leeds.

190. There was double trouble for Sunderland and Aston Villa when the strike force of Peter Davenport *(above)* and Trevor Christie got together in September 1985. Davenport got a hat-trick to beat Sunderland; Christie followed up four days later with one of his own at Villa Park.

191. Of all the overseas players, two Dutchmen were the most successful. Hans van Breukelen (with boss Brian Clough and defender Paul Hart) had the daunting task of replacing Peter Shilton. He did it brilliantly, until PSV Eindhoven lured him back home in May 1984.

192. Signed from Real Madrid, Johnny Metgod (pictured here wit his son Dimitri) claimed one of the most explosive goals ever see at the City Ground when he fired in a 25-yard free kick agains West Ham.

193-194. *above:* Frans Thijssen who spent less than a season at Forest. *right:* Brian Clough and the other two players signed on the same day, Gary Megson (*left*) and Franz Carr. *below:* Raimondo Ponte who was sold to Monaco after only 21 League appearances. *below right:* Norwegian Eina Aas with his central defensive partner Kenny Burns.

195. Australian Alan Davidson (with Ron Fenton) at least experienced his first heavy snowfall at Forest; but illness and injury eventually meant he had to return home.

196. Norwegian Kjetil Osvold went back to Scandinavia, to Swedi club Djurgaarden after less than a half a dozen matches in twelv months.

197. So near and yet ... Forest are beaten 2-1 in the FA Cup semi finals by Liverpool at Hillsborough. Nigel Clough, sandwiched by Alan Hansen and Bruce Grobbelaar, pulls a goal back from close range.

198. A superb finish by John Aldridge ends an equally fine move between John Barnes and Peter Beardsley.

199. Colin Foster climbs above Hansen in the semi-final.

200. The same two players fight for possession again, alongside Gary Gillespie and Paul Wilkinson.

201. The prize guys, captain Johnny Metgod receives the County Cup after a 2-0 win over Notts County in May 1986. Alongside him are *(from left to right)* Garry Birtles, Notts FA chairman John Crampton, Steve Sutton and Stuart Pearce.

202. The indoor champions of England: The Forest squad after winning the Guinness Soccer Six Championship at the G-Mex Centre in Manchester in December 1987. Forest beat Manchester United on penalties in the final of the two night event. The winning smiles from *(left to right)*: Graham Lyas (physio), Ron Fenton, Nigel Clough, Steve Sutton, Calvin Plummer, Lee Glover, Liam O'Kane, Alan Clarke. *front row*: Tommy Gaynor, Colin Foster, Stuart Pearce, Gary Charles, Darren Wassall, Neil Webb.

203. Paul Wilkinson's explosive goal against Arsenal in the FA Cup quarter finals.

204. Off duty and on it: Neil Webb finds life at the wicket a bit claustrophobic as Forest train with bat and ball *(from left to right)* Des Walker, David Campbell, Phil Starbuck, Gary Mills, Brett Williams, Johnny Metgod, Steve Sutton, Ian Bowyer, Gary Fleming, Hans Segers.

205. On yer bike: the Forest squad 1980-81 *(from left to right)*: John Robertson, Justin Fashanu, John McGovern, Bryn Gunn, Stuart Gray, Einar Aas, Mark Proctor, Peter Ward, Viv Anderson, Kenny Burns, David Needham, Peter Shilton, Ian Wallace, Gary Mills.

206. The squad which took Forest to the semi-finals of the UEFA Cup in 1983-84. *back row, from left to right:* Colin Walsh, Viv Anderson, Peter Davenport, Garry Birtles, Bryn Gunn. *middle row:* Ron Fenton, Danny Wilson, Steve Sutton, Hans Van Breukelen, Paul Hart, Brian Clough. *front row:* Colin Todd, Steve Hodge, Kenny Swain, Ian Bowyer, Steve Wigley, Ian Wallace, Chris Fairclough.

207. Forest pull off a Championship win: The Central League. Tommy Gaynor scores the second of his two goals in a 2-0 win over Liverpool at the City Ground which virtually wrapped up the title.

208. The champagne flows in the dressing room after Forest have beaten Aston Villa 6-0 at Villa Park (including a Gaynor hat trick) to confirm the Championship. *back row,(left to right*: Gary Parker, Nigel Jemson, Tommy Gaynor, Brian Rice, Brett Williams, Lee Glover, Tony Abrahams. *middle row:* Gary Charles, Colin Foster, Liam O'Kane, Darren Wassall, Gary Andrews, Phil Starbuck, Mark Crossley. *front row*: Alan Lamb, Terry Wilson, Steve Chettle, Hans Segers, Archie Gemmill, Steve McLoughlin.

209. Wembley winners again: Forest celebrate the Football League's 100th birthday by clinching the Mercantile Credit trophy.

210 & 211. Flying high: Carr, in the second round of the Mercantile Credit Trophy against Leeds.

212. Forest, after beating Sheffield Wednesday 3-2 on penalties in the final. *back row, left to right*: Nigel Jemson, Terry Wilson, Nigel Clough, Steve Sutton, Lee Glover, Mark Crossley, Gary Parker, Gary Brown, Gary Charles, Gary Crosby, Darren Wassall, Colin Foster. *front row*: Steve Chettle, Tommy Gaynor, Brian Rice, Stuart Pearce, Franz Carr, Neil Webb, Gary Fleming.

213. I'm dreaming of the First Division. Gary Crosby *(extreme right)* cost just £15,000 when Forest signed him from Beazer Homes League side, Grantham (on the recommendation of Martin O'Neill, the manager). Within two months the former joiner was in the side and on his way to an FA Cup semi final. Inevitably, he earned the nickname 'Bing' - hence the straw hat and the chorus line of Neil Webb, Steve Chettle, Calvin Plummer and Stuart Pearce.

4. Neil Webb - after signing a
w contract.

215. Syd Owen, saking hands and exchanging pennants with Jack Burkitt, was named Footballer of the Year a few days before the 1959 FA Cup final.

Acknowledgements

This is not - and was never intended to be - a kick by kick account of Nottingham Forest over the last 30 or so years. There was insufficient time and space to compile a complete history, something which has already been admirably covered by John Lawson, Keith Mellor and A J Turner. It's merely my intention to bring back a few memories about the highlights, now and again adding a bit of interpretation and including a few lesser known stories, particularly around the photographs themselves.

But to pharaphrase John Donne: No author is an island. This book could not have been written without the patience, tolerance and talent of others. In the *Evening Post* photographic department, Ron Braisby was indispensable and always sympathetic, despite almost daily enquiries from yours truly. Without him, there would have been an awful lot of white space to fill. In the *Post* library, Colin Panter gave incalculable assistance from day one. Dennis Marshall (an expert on both sides of the River Trent) came to my rescue by generously lending his own album of photographs and then willingly gave his time to tell the tale behind them. Trevor Frecknall acted as proof reader on every page (in other words, any errors belong to him) and John Lawson answered many questions . Of course, the book would not have been possible without those people in the firing line - the photographers. The luxury of writing about something is being able to change it. The gentleman with the camera is not so fortunate. He can hardly ask a centre forward if he'd mind scoring his goal again because the lens was a bit misty or the light was wrong. Courtesy of Nottingham Forest's success on the continent, I had the pleasure of going on a tour of Europe with Trevor Bartlett and, while he always managed to find the worst restaurant in whichever city we happened to be in at the time, his photographs were always of the finest quality. The contribution of his colleauges has been every bit as invaluable to me. My thanks go to: the perceptive Richard Denning, David Baird (particularly for so superbly capturing both headers from Nigel Clough in the final chapter), Bill Greenhoff, Robert Simpson, John Richardson (for the 'Pathway to Promotion'), Steve Footitt, Kate Blatchford and Nicholas Forman Hardy. For permission to reproduce other photographs free of charge I am indebted to Raymonds News Agency at Derby, Charlie Noble, Paul Lewis of Manchester, Malcolm Hepple, picture editor of the *Coventry Evening Telegraph* and Alan Oliver of the *Newcastle Evening Chronicle*. Brian Clough and Maurice Roworth kindly wrote a message and the forward respectively and, over the years, have always been immensely helpful. Billy Gray gave me a considerable amount of background material to the 1959 FA Cup win. As regards research, Ralph Gee supplied me with the newspaper cuttings he kept throughout the Championship and European Cup winning years. Design by Clive Hardy; cover by Lorraine Shaw; editorial by Liz Weekes.